HOW TO COMPLAIN

How to Complain: The Consumer Guide to Cancelling Parking Tickets and Winning Pothole Claims

By Scott Dixon
www.thecomplaintsresolver.co.uk

Copyright © Scott Dixon, 2023

This book is sold subject to the condition that it shall not, by way of trade or otherwise, be lent, resold, hired out, or otherwise circulated without the publisher's prior consent in any form of binding or cover other than that in which it is published and without a similar condition including this condition being imposed on the subsequent publisher.

No portion of this book may be copied, retransmitted, reposted, duplicated or otherwise used without the express written approval of the author.

Although the author and publisher have made every effort to ensure that the information in this book was correct at the time of being published, the author and publisher do not assume and hereby disclaim any liability to any party for any loss or damage caused by errors or omissions.

DISCLAIMER: This book is not intended as a substitute for legal advice. The specific facts that apply to your case may result in a different outcome than the case studies specified here.

The moral right of Scott Dixon has been asserted.

FOREWORD

As a fellow Consumer Champion with an exemplary in-depth knowledge of every single rule and regulation you could ever think of, Scott Dixon is undoubtedly the 'go to' man for any kind of consumer issue. This is clearly demonstrated in the first of his books 'How to Complain – The Consumer Guide to Resolve Complaints and Motoring Disputes' where Scott advises how to effectively complain in order to achieve appropriate redress and refunds for poor service.

In this equally impressive and comprehensive follow up, Scott takes a look at how to deal specifically with parking tickets and pothole complaints and with his usual sharp eye skilfully advises how to make short work of organisations who see motorists as an easy ride.

If you read this book then no parking ticket or pothole will ever phase you again because with its straight to the point templates and easy to follow instructions, you will have the tools with which to hold authorities to account, seek compensation, file successful claims and win appeals.

Knowledge is power. Use it.

Lady Janey

Consumer Expert

www.ladyjaney.co.uk

www.facebook.com/ladyjaney75

www.twitter.com/ladyjaney75

www.instagram.com/ladyjaney75

www.pinterest.com/ladyjaney75

www.linkedin.com/ladyjaney75

ACKNOWLEDGEMENTS

I would like to thank my followers on my Facebook page The Complaints Resolver, customers, friends and family for their support and encouragement on this journey to date. I never realised when I began writing my first book that I would come this far with interviews and features with BBC Radio Scotland, Daily Mail, Which? Conversation, BBC Breakfast and Newsweek.

To be acknowledged and recognised as 1 of 5 of the best consumer champions in the UK is an achievement I am proud of.

I am pleased to say that I have made a significant difference to the lives of many consumers by raising awareness of consumer rights and how to seek redress. That is the cornerstone of what I do and this book will give you the same tools as I have to get results every time.

I have other books and projects in the pipeline and I look forward to engaging with you in years to come.

CONTENTS

INTRODUCTION 9
CHAPTER 1 – PARKING TICKETS ISSUED BY LOCAL AUTHORITIES 11
CHAPTER 2 – PARKING ON PRIVATE LAND 21
CHAPTER 3 – WAYS TO CANCEL A PARKING TICKET 35
CHAPTER 4 – REASONS TO APPEAL 39
CHAPTER 5 – INVITATION TO TREAT 47
CHAPTER 6 – HOW TO WIN YOUR APPEAL 49
CHAPTER 7 – THE DIFFERENCE BETWEEN DEBT COLLECTORS AND BAILIFFS 51
CHAPTER 8 – COURT HEARINGS 53
CHAPTER 9 – HOW TO SUE A PARKING FIRM 57
CHAPTER 10 – GENERAL DATA PROTECTION REGULATION ACT 2018 63
CHAPTER 11 – HOW TO FILE A SMALL CLAIM IN COURT 71
CHAPTER 12 – HOW TO SEEK COMPENSATION FOR POTHOLE DAMAGE 81
USEFUL CONTACTS 99

INTRODUCTION

The inspiration behind writing this book is simply because I often get asked questions about private parking tickets and appeals.

It is such a complex and grey area that is not regulated and revolves around contract law, and few people understand the differences between official parking tickets issued by local authorities and tickets issued by private parking firms.

It is clearly profitable and motorists are just seen as easy pickings because they do not understand how to tackle this scourge. I have decided to shine a spotlight on this topic to simplify it, clarify your rights and how you can fight back against it.

The law differs right across the British Isles, so I have looked at how you can deal with parking tickets in Scotland, England and Wales, Northern Ireland and the Isle of Man.

I explain the difference between parking tickets issued by local authorities and private parking firms, various ways to cancel a parking ticket, how to lodge and win an appeal, the General Data Protection Regulation Act 2018 and how to sue for breaches and damages based on your data (which belongs to you) being misused by private parking firms.

The final section covers pothole claims and how you can easily hold the authorities to account, as this is another plague that blights motorists.

I hope you find this an interesting and useful read.

CHAPTER 1 – PARKING TICKETS ISSUED BY LOCAL AUTHORITIES

Not many people contest a parking ticket, yet if you do so in the UK and the Isle of Man, the odds are stacked in your favour of winning an appeal so it is worth considering. Furthermore, if the Council do not adhere to their timelines on the appeals process, you can get the ticket cancelled on that basis.

The Consumer Rights Act that came in to effect on 1 October 2015 now provides motorists with a 10-minute grace period after a ticket has expired. This covers the end of free and paid parking across the whole of the UK (excluding the Isle of Man) and also applies to council run car parks.

Council parking controls have to be enshrined in bylaws, called Traffic Regulation Orders. The signs and markings used to impose the restrictions have to be displayed and painted according to Department for Transport instructions before tickets can be issued, with only 'minor deviations' allowed.

The Regulations applying to these signs are called the Traffic Signs Regulations and General Directions 2002, although Section 2 of this legislation was revoked on 22 April 2016.

This means that there is no requirement for any highway authority to place speed limit signs anywhere on the highway.

There are no test cases in Court at the time of writing to see if this will be challenged by drivers pleading 'Not Guilty' as a result of not being given adequate guidance, or any guidance at all, of the speed limit in force on a particular stretch of road.

Chapter 5 of The Traffic Signs Manual Road Markings 2003 is the legislation that local authorities are supposed to adhere to, and the link is as follows:

www.gov.uk/government/uploads/system/uploads/attachment_data/file/223667/trafficsigns-manual-chapter-05.pdf

It contains 162 pages and is probably ideal for bed-time reading! If signs and markings are unclear, they are unlawful, and council parking attendants are not trained to recognise incorrect signs.

You need to collate as much evidence as possible at the scene where the ticket was issued and act fast if you wish to appeal. The key is to question the legality and cast reasonable doubt on the alleged offence to win your case.

Whatever you do, do not pay the fine and appeal afterwards. Payment is considered an admission of liability so your case will be closed with no options to appeal.

If you appeal within 14 days, the 50% discount that applies to early payment will be frozen.

Motorists who lose their case must pay the full fine, forfeiting the 50% discount for those who pay early. If still unpaid after 28 days, local authorities can issue a charge certificate which raises the cost by 50%.

The main reasons you may wish to appeal with a good chance of success are as follows:

The contravention did not occur as:

- the ticket was issued within a ten minute 'grace' period
- the signs were either unclear or misleading
- the road markings are broken or not visible
- snow or heavy rain made the markings inconspicuous
- the ticket was not issued

There are spelling mistakes or typing errors on the parking ticket. It cannot be said that it was you that contravened the regulations if the ticket has not been issued correctly.

The council states that the ticket was issued by post as the traffic warden was prevented from issuing the ticket, but you did not receive it.

The vehicle was stolen, or you have sold the car and can evidence that you were not the legal owner, when the alleged contravention took place.

The Traffic Regulation Order was invalid by virtue of the council adding new restrictions without following correct procedures.

There were mitigating circumstances such as an emergency, health problem, your vehicle breaking down or having fear for your own safety.

Take photos at the scene with a focus on road signs or markings, if this is the reason why you wish to contest the legality of the parking ticket.

Road signs and markings must be clearly visible by day and by night.

The lack of maintenance of yellow lines signifying parking restrictions is a legitimate reason to cancel a parking ticket. Breaks in a yellow line, or if they are not correctly terminated at the ends, mean that a yellow line cannot be enforced, even though it ought to be fairly clear that parking is restricted.

Follow the appeals procedure and provide as much evidence as possible to support your claim.

You need to enclose a couple of photos casting reasonable doubt on the legality of the issued fixed penalty notice and refuse to pay the fine based on the photographic evidence. Also state that you have other photos which you will produce in Court if your appeal is rejected.

If the road markings and/or signs are so poorly marked, the local authority is not in a solid position to reject your appeal and risks racking up costs by taking it to Court. This would also potentially attract adverse publicity, especially on social media.

After all, you are not a mind reader and the local authority cannot expect people to pay fines if they cannot be bothered to employ people to keep the road markings clear. A fine is not enforceable if the road markings are not clear and do not comply with the prescribed layout enshrined in law.

Compliance with the Road Traffic Act cuts both ways. Your claim will be heard by an independent panel, and these individuals have probably been in the same position as you over the years. If you present your case with solid evidence and are reasonable, you stand a good chance of winning your case.

If you lose at this stage, you can take it further to an independent tribunal but you need to carefully consider the costs and whether it is worth it.

All I will say is that honesty is the best policy and do not lie if you choose to contest a parking fine, as you will need to evidence your claim and you risk being prosecuted for attempting to pervert the course of justice.

A legitimate parking ticket that is issued is not worth lying for as you could end up with a criminal record.

The template to contest a parking fine in the UK is as follows (amend to suit):

Dear Sir/Madam

Subject: Penalty Charge Notice/Fixed Penalty Notice [delete as applicable] [reference details] [date]

I write to you in respect of the above Penalty Charge Notice issued to my vehicle in [full address] on [date].

I have examined the Parking Bay/Sign/Yellow Line [delete as appropriate] in relation to the penalty you have issued and I find that the markings on the highway fail to meet the legal requirements as set out in Statute and Regulations.

I therefore intend to appeal against the parking ticket issued to me at [location] on [date]. I request that your authority therefore provide me with details of:

The Traffic Penalty Tribunal
The Local Government Ombudsman

I also ask that you formally record my appeal against the fixed penalty ticket.

I am aware that a 'traffic sign' is the only form of signing that a highway authority is empowered to place on a road to direct traffic, and any other form of sign positioned by you cannot in any way be made to resemble a 'traffic sign'.

Also, if the sign chosen or provided by a Highway Authority for the purpose of directing drivers as to what (if any) restriction applies does not meet the strict criteria set out in *law, then the sign is 'non-prescribed'. The Government sets out that the use of 'non-prescribed' signs on a highway is illegal, and an authority who chooses to use such signs is 'acting beyond its powers'.*

I am also aware that your highway engineers are provided with clear guidance on the provision of such lines and bays within Chapter 3 and Chapter 5 of the Traffic Signs Manual, both of which confirm the correct marking of a highway.

Whilst there tends to be a belief amongst some that a sign has merely to be recognisable as a sign to apply a restriction, the Case of Davies v Heatley 1971 directs that even if a sign is clearly recognisable to a man as being a sign of that kind, if it does conform to regulations no offence is committed.

Your authority has a clear duty in law, having access to relevant legislation, Government guidance and advice and your own Legal Department. It is clear to me that the failure to place signs to prescribed requirements must therefore be a conscious decision.

You are no doubt aware that you would be advised not to enforce defective lines and signs as they would invalidate the ticket issued. I therefore suggest that the decision to enforce defective restrictions must also be a conscious choice to act in breach of the law.

In essence, I do not accept that the parking restrictions imposed on [street name] are lawful, that the ticket issued is therefore invalid and the actions of the authority are in full knowledge of the breach of law and their legal obligations.

I take this opportunity to notify you that it is my intention to:

appeal the Penalty Charge Notice to the Parking Adjudication Service

make a formal complaint to the Local Government Ombudsman

I enclose photos to support my appeal for your perusal.

I welcome any comments you may have, and I look forward to hearing from you soon.

Yours faithfully

Northern Ireland

The website to contest parking fines issued by local authorities is www.courtsni.gov.uk and it provides contact details for 17 provinces within Northern Ireland with links to forms, services and publications.

Isle of Man

A request for a review of any fixed penalty notice issued by local authorities must be made in writing to:

Parking Administration
Department of Infrastructure
Sea Terminal Building
Douglas
Isle of Man IM1 2RF

Ensure that you quote the fixed penalty notice number and your car registration details. You can expect to receive a response within ten days on receipt of your appeal.

You can request a Court hearing if your appeal is rejected by writing to:

The Parking Section
Sea Terminal Building
Douglas
Isle of Man
IM1 2RF

Alternatively, you can send an e-mail to: parkingfines.doi@gov.im or complete the Request for Court hearing on the form attached to the Notice to Owner letter.

All the paperwork will be prepared and forwarded to the Isle of Man Courts who will then contact you directly with a Court date.

CHAPTER 2 – PARKING ON PRIVATE LAND

The first thing to understand here is that a private parking company cannot fine you. They can only issue invoices disguised as a fine for a breach of contract for parking on private land.

The invoices are deliberately made to look like a local authority Penalty Charge Notice (PCN), but are called a **Parking** Charge Notice.

This flourishing industry is not supported by any legislation and relies on contract law. The signs create and form binding contracts setting out the Terms and Conditions and motorists accept this by parking on the private land.

It is not a crime to park in a private car park and you cannot be taken to a Criminal Court, although you can be pursued through Civil Courts.

If you appeal and its rejected, the private parking operator still offers the discount rate.

However, if they reject your appeal and you still appeal to PoPLA, you lose the discount so there is no harm in lodging an appeal.

There is no Keeper Liability in Scotland and Northern Ireland (yet), although this is set to change before the end of 2023 (TBC). This means that they cannot be enforced unless you respond to confirm who is responsible. Nevertheless, this doesn't give you permission to repeatedly ignore parking rules on private land.

This means that only the driver is liable. As you don't have to respond as the keeper and identify the driver, you can simply refuse to respond.

The Protection of Freedoms Act (PoFA) applies in England and Wales only. This means that the registered keeper is liable for any parking charges for the vehicle.

You enter in to a contract with the landowner when you park your car in a private car park such as those in supermarkets and hospitals.

Car park signs which set out the terms of the contract that you have entered in to need to be clearly visible and easy to interpret.

Any breaches may result in the PCN being sent to the registered keeper of the vehicle and the parking firm will have obtained your details from the DVLA. The onus is on the parking firm to prove that the registered keeper of the vehicle was driving the vehicle at the time the breach occurred.

The car park operator cannot recover the money without taking Court action, and you can refer any member firms that pester you demanding settlement of any invoices to the British Parking Association (BPA) or the Independent Parking Committee (IPC) if they are members.

These are the only parking trade associations in the UK and have a Code of Practice for their members to abide by, yet in reality motorists remain vulnerable to unfair practices.

The British Parking Association (BPA) is a trade association which is fully funded by its members. It is the only association which represents the parking industry throughout the UK. Most of the local Government organisations, Healthcare Trusts, train operators and theme parks are members.

Parking firms that are members of the British Parking Association Limited (which are members of the Accredited Trade Association) have to follow their Code of Practice, which means that they can access the DVLA's database of registered keepers.

You can check the British Parking Association's website www.britishparking.co.uk to see if an operator is a member. Firms which are members of the British Parking Association (BPA) include:

- Parking Eye Limited
  www.parkingeye.co.uk

- Parkopedia Limited
  www.parkopedia.co.uk

- UK Parking Control Limited
  www.ukparkingcontrol.com

- Euro Car Parks
  www.eurocarparks.com

Most of the local councils and authorities are members.

The parking firm can get the name and address of a registered keeper from the DVLA and send a demand for payment.

Private parking companies who **are not** members of the BPA or IPC cannot access the DVLA database and simply rely on motorists paying the invoice affixed to their windscreen. They therefore have no means of identifying anyone to settle their invoices and are not able to pursue you to pay it. You can therefore ignore the tickets.

The only way they can obtain your details is if you write to the parking firm to contest the parking ticket and provide them with your name and address.

If you receive a private parking ticket on your windscreen, wait until one comes by post. The private parking operator does not know who the Keeper is and rely on you contacting them appealing it to find out.

If you are an Isle of Man resident driving in the UK, you do not need to respond to any private parking tickets as the private parking operators will not have access to the Manx registered keeper database to find out who owns the vehicle.

They will also not have jurisdiction to pursue it through the Isle of Man Courts, nor will they do so for a trivial amount.

Notice to Driver
A Notice to Driver is a ticket placed on the windscreen at the time of the alleged parking contravention.

If you receive a Notice to Driver ticket, you are advised to wait until you receive a Notice to Keeper letter. These are time-set and must be delivered between 28 – 56 days after the ticket was issued. Parking firms that are not members of the BPA or IPC are likely not to have access to the DVLA database of registered keepers, so they do not know your address.

The exception to this rule is if you are driving a hire car or your vehicle is on a Personal Contract Plan (PCP). You will need to contact the parking firm as soon as possible to prevent letters going to the hire company and having charges taken from your credit / debit card. You will need to appeal as the keeper in these scenarios.

Registered Keeper
A Notice to Keeper is a ticket sent and received by post.

The Protection of Freedoms Act 2012 only requires the registered keeper to tell the driver and give the notice to the driver.

The issue date of the invoice to keeper ought to be issued within 14 days of the parking incident and alleged breach of contract. This is to give you time to challenge it. Never admit to being the driver. If it is issued after 14 days, it is invalid.

Parking firms have no statutory powers to force the registered keeper of the vehicle to provide the name and address of the driver. The parking firm only has the power to invite the registered keeper to provide the name and address of the driver under regulation 9(2)(e) of Schedule 4 of the Protection of Freedoms Act 2012.

Appeal as the keeper and refuse to disclose who the driver is.

The template to do so is as follows:

Date:

Reference: PCN xxx

Dear Sir / Madam,

Many thanks for your recent correspondence.

Since your Notice to Keeper did not arrive until xx days after the parking incident, it does not therefore comply with the Protection of Freedoms Act 2012 (POFA 2012) and as such there is no keeper's liability.

I am sure you are aware with ANPR camera systems the Notice to Keeper (NTK) has to be received within 14 days.

You may not assume that I, the keeper, was the driver on this day.

There is no need to place this PCN on hold as I am not obliged to name the driver and will not do so.

You can issue a code for accessing a suitable appeal process if you choose to persist in this manner. This will be utilised in full.

Please forward an appeal code or cancel the invoice if you wish.

Yours faithfully,

The keeper of the vehicle will continue to receive a series of threatening letters upping the ante if the driver refuses to pay the invoice.

The onus and burden of proof lies with the parking firm to prove that you breached the terms and conditions of the contract you entered in to in parking on private land.

Parking firms will always be liable for their legal fees when they commence legal proceedings regardless of the outcome. This is the risk they take and makes a defended claim commercially uneconomical.

They rely on you not defending the claim and securing a default judgement against you. If you do not put a reasonable defence forward, you cannot apply to set the judgement aside.

Parking on Private Land Appeals (PoPLA) is the independent appeals service set up by the British Parking Association.

PoPLA will only investigate appeals from members of the British Parking Association as a last resort if your appeal through the operator's internal complaints procedure has failed. You will need the verification code to appeal online or when sending in your appeal form by post otherwise it will not be considered. PoPLA has an Independent Scrutiny Board and is transparent insofar as it publishes an Annual Report declaring the number of appeals and nature of decisions.

Over 50% of appeals made to PoPLA are upheld, which evidences my suspicions that local authorities and private parking firms are just playing the percentages game knowing that 28% of motorists simply pay up even if they believe that they have done nothing wrong.

The International Parking Community (IPC) is a competitor to the British Parking Association.

The Independent Appeals Service (IAS) hears appeals from motorists who have received tickets from its members anywhere in the UK. The main difference here is that they are not transparent, whereas PoPLA is.

Scotland

There is no keeper liability in Scotland so contract law applies.

You may be sent a ticket if you are the registered keeper of a vehicle who has breached the terms and conditions set by the parking firm. However, you are under no obligation to identify the driver of the vehicle at the time of the alleged contravention.

There is no Keeper Liability in Scotland and Northern Ireland (yet), although this is set to change before the end of 2023 (TBC). This means that they cannot be enforced unless you respond to confirm who is responsible. Nevertheless, this doesn't give you permission to repeatedly ignore parking rules on private land.

A precedent has been set in Scotland on this matter. One individual in Dundee was found liable to pay £24,500 in 2017 after ignoring countless £100 a day invoices (Vehicle Control Services v Carly Mackie, Dundee Sheriff Court, 13 January 2017). It was proved in Court that Vehicle Control Services clearly displayed signs which advised of the consequences of parking a vehicle without a permit. This formed the basis of the contract. By continually choosing to park without a permit, she had accepted the terms and conditions and breached the contract.

When you enter private land and park in a space, you are entering in to a binding contract with the landowner. The contract is between the landowner and the driver of the vehicle – not the registered keeper. A contract does not have to be in writing.

Any breach of the contract may result in you being issued with an invoice disguised as a parking fine.

The onus is on the landowner or parking firm acting on their behalf to prove on the balance of probabilities that the person they are suing for a breach of contract was the driver of the vehicle when it was parked in their car park.

If it is proved that the driver breached the contract, the driver is liable to pay damages. A precedent has been set in the Supreme Court in the case of Parking Eye Limited v Beavis (2015) UKSC 67. The Supreme Court is the highest ruling Court in the UK and all rulings here apply throughout the UK.

This case ruled that an £85 charge was not unreasonable and discounted previous claims that the landowners could only sue for what they estimated they had lost because of a car being parked on their land. It is virtually impossible to prove that a landowner had lost money due to a vehicle being parked in a parking space and this argument does not apply.

All private parking tickets that are issued are not automatically enforceable. A landowner or the car parking firm operating on their behalf must still prove that a contract existed and who actually breached that contract.

Northern Ireland

The driver of the vehicle is liable for any private parking invoices – not the registered keeper. The parking firm may write to the registered keeper asking / demanding the details of the driver and payment of the invoice, but the keeper is not obliged to do so.

You can state, as the keeper of the vehicle, that you are not liable for any costs and you are not prepared to disclose who the driver was and you are not obliged to do so.

Private parking firms can clamp you on private land. This has been outlawed everywhere else across the UK.

The onus is on the private parking firm to prove who committed the breach of contract, not you. The Consumer Council will contact the firm on your behalf as the registered keeper of the vehicle to seek evidence that the PCN has been issued to the driver on the date of the alleged breach.

You should contact the Consumer Council immediately if you have received a Parking Charge Notice (PCN) from a private parking firm.

All private parking firms need to adhere to the British Parking Association's Code of Practice. The Consumer Council can check to see that the PCN has been properly issued and is able to challenge it if not.

The Consumer Council will request that the invoice is cancelled if the parking firm cannot provide the required evidence.

The Consumer Council can be contacted on 0800 121 6022 or by email: contact@consumercouncil.org.uk

If You Have Been Clamped
Do not try and remove the clamp as you could be held liable for criminal damage.

Any firm using clampers needs to have a 16-digit licence number issued by the Security Industry Authority (SIA). Ask for the number and verify it on www.sla.homeoffice.gov.uk

Template to contest a private parking ticket in Northern Ireland

Dear Sir/Madam

Subject: Parking Charge Notice [reference details] [date of issue] [vehicle registration]

I write to you in respect of the above Parking Charge Notice issued to my vehicle in [full address] on [date].

I shall not be paying your demand for payment as I was not the driver of the vehicle at the time of the alleged contravention. I am under no obligation to disclose who was driving the vehicle so please do not contact me again in respect of this matter.

Please be aware that I shall consider any more correspondence from you to be harassment and I shall report you to the Police / British Parking Association / Independent Parking Committee / the Security Industry Authority (if the firm is a member of any of these bodies) if you contact me again.

Yours faithfully
(Enclose all relevant evidence)

CHAPTER 3 – WAYS TO CANCEL A PARKING TICKET

Gather your evidence

Take photographs of any signs, where your vehicle was parked, road markings and keep your parking ticket and any supplementary evidence.

Try and find any witnesses that are prepared to support you with your case.

Go straight to the landowner

The key weapon in your arsenal is to avoid the ticket company and go straight to the landowner. For example, if you get a ticket while parking at Morrisons, you should complain to Morrisons direct or their Head Office.

If you know who the landowner is, contact them and they will often cancel the ticket for you. They don't want the bad publicity, complaints, adverse press coverage and negative online reviews.

Asda will cancel parking tickets within 24 hours and Aldi and Lidl are also good at cancelling tickets.

Always get confirmation in writing.

Ignore the time conditions

Ignore the time conditions on the ticket about discounts in settling it straight away. Do not rush in to doing anything and forget about the discount. Payment may be considered as an admission of liability without further recourse to appeal.

Never admit to being the owner
If you enter in to correspondence with the parking ticket company, always refer to the 'keeper' of the car and never the actual owner. Never say 'I' or 'we'. This empowers you on the negotiations.

There is no Keeper Liability in Scotland and Northern Ireland (yet), although this is set to change before the end of 2023 (TBC). This means that they cannot be enforced unless you respond to confirm who is responsible. Nevertheless, this doesn't give you permission to repeatedly ignore parking rules on private land.

This means that only the driver is liable. As you don't have to respond as the keeper and identify the driver, you can simply refuse to respond.

Keeper Liability allows proceedings against the registered keeper when the creditor (usually the landowner or their agent the parking operator) does not know who the driver was at the time of the parking incident.

Never reveal who the driver of the car was. Do not ring the parking ticket company and reveal that you were driving the car. Wait until a ticket arrives in the post. It is always best practice not to reveal your details. The parking firms do not know the identity of the driver so they rely on you disclosing it.

This does not apply to lease cars or penalty charges in railway car parks though. So, if your car is on a PCP plan, bear that in mind as it is effectively on a lease agreement.

What to do if your case has been passed to debt collectors

You may need professional help here. However, the clock can be reset by looking at legal precedents such as Ferguson -v- British Gas here in 2009.

Ms Ferguson ('the claimant') had been a customer of British Gas and had changed suppliers. British Gas subjected the claimant to a constant stream of threatening letters despite being asked to put a stop to it on numerous occasions by lodging complaints. British Gas assured her that they would but didn't.

Ms Ferguson took British Gas to Court for harassment and won her case. The Court upheld her claim of harassment and that it fell within the remit of The Protection from Harassment Act 1997, and that it was likely that she would suffer real anxiety and distress by the threatening actions of British Gas.

British Gas tried to downplay the seriousness of it by saying that the letters were computer generated, which was contested on the basis that real people are responsible for creating the programmes and entering them in to the computers to create the letters.

All appeals by British Gas failed and the case was upheld.

An alternative approach you can take is to contact the car park operator as soon as possible if you believe that the fine is excessive and you have been unfairly penalised, and provide as much information as possible such as:

- Photos of any misleading signs

- Circumstances
- Car registration and parking fine reference

You may also wish to speak to the landowner and make them aware of the company's conduct and how it is adversely affecting their business.

The car park operator cannot recover the money without taking Court action, and you can refer any member firms that pester you demanding settlement of any fines to the British Parking Association (BPA) or the Independent Parking Committee (IPC) if they are members.

CHAPTER 4 – REASONS TO APPEAL

The invoice is disproportionate to the breach (is it fair to issue a £100 invoice to someone for overstaying by a few minutes in a free car park?)

The charge is too high (maximum set can be up to £100)

You were parked correctly within the time allowed.

The road markings are broken or not visible.

Parking rules and signs are unclear, hidden or obscured with misleading wording. If signs are difficult to read, not present or misleading, it cannot be said that the car park was adequately signed therefore the contract is null and void.

The sign is incapable of being read in ambient light at night. You therefore have an unreadable sign which, in itself, is not capable of forming a contract. Therefore, there is no breach and the Notice to Keeper (NTK) is not compliant.

No CCTV or Automatic Number Plate Recognition (ANPR) signs in place.

ANPR cameras may not have planning permission.

Associated signs may not have planning consent.

Signs larger than 0.3 square metres require express consent from the Local Planning Authority.

Private parking firms are duty bound to comply with the law in creating and enforcing contracts with a driver or keeper of a vehicle, and in conveying the terms of the contract.

No way to pay. If the parking meter is broken and there are no alternative payment methods available, it cannot be said that you entered into and breached a contract.

You were not the driver of the vehicle.

You have broken down. You cannot be expected to move a broken-down vehicle to adhere to parking rules.

You used the café or other supermarket facilities after you did your shop.

You are elderly and / or disabled and you would take longer to buy a ticket and use the facilities.

The Equality Act 2010 requires reasonable adjustments to be made and you can use this to successfully appeal a ticket on the grounds of discrimination.

You have genuine mitigating circumstances such as an illness or mental health issues.

You accidentally inputted the wrong registration details in to the parking machine. It is not an offence if you incorrectly type in a wrong registration. Proof of purchase is all that is required and this can be evidenced by the ANPR / CCTV records or by taking photos with your smartphone.

These machines do not make allowances for people with dyslexia. Dyslexia is a protected characteristic under the

Equality Act 2010 and the NHS estimates that up to 10% of the population suffers from some form of it.

You have made more than one visit to a supermarket car park and have been issued with a ticket based upon the first entry and final exit (often referred to as a double dip).

The parking firm has to send a ticket to the keeper's current address within 14 days of the alleged parking contravention in accordance with the Protection of Freedoms Act 2012. This includes weekends and bank holidays. If the ticket was sent a few weeks / months afterwards, you can appeal as keeper without naming the driver as it is invalid (see template on page 26).

The signage may not have advertising consent or planning permission.

Has the landowner given permission to the operator to enforce the parking charges? Is there a contract in place? Parking charges can only be made if the signage is correct. Otherwise, it can be viewed as an 'invitation to treat' and not be a legally binding contract.

KADOE (Keeper at Date of Event) contract and the Code of Practice that member firms sign up to and agree to adhere to require that the operator has to have authority from the landowner to issue and enforce parking tickets.

If this is not in place, this is a clear breach and misuse of your personal data under the General Data Protection Regulation Act (GDPR) 2018.

You were not the keeper of the vehicle at the time of the alleged contravention (you had sold it or it had been stolen).

You did not break the rules.

You had a good reason.

Template to appeal a private parking ticket in England and Wales for private parking firms that are members of the British Parking Association Limited's Approved Operator Scheme (amend to suit)

Without prejudice, except as to costs
Subject: Parking Charge Notice – Notice to Keeper [reference details] [date of issue] [vehicle registration]

I write to you in respect of the above Parking Charge Notice – Notice to Keeper issued to my vehicle in [full address] on [date].

I would be grateful if you could answer all of my questions below and address the issues raised before I decide how to proceed with your Parking Charge Notice. I shall be able to make an informed decision on how I wish to proceed on receipt of your answers.

I dispute your claim for the reasons listed below. My primary concern is the disproportionate and excessive amount of your parking charge, which I ask that you justify.

1. ***Your parking charge amount***

    Please clarify on which of the following grounds your claim is based:

    Damages for trespass

    Damages for breach of contract

    A contractual sum

2. **Your loss**

   If your case is based on damages for trespass or a breach of contract, please provide me with a full breakdown of the actual losses incurred which are truly represented in the damages you are claiming for as caused by the alleged parking contravention.

3. **Your status – the creditor**

   Your Parking Charge Notice simply names (parking firm). Please advise me who is the actual creditor, who is making the claim and in what capacity.

4. **Landowner**

   Please advise me who owns the car park so I can send them a copy of this letter.

5. **Contractual Authority (as required by BPA Limited AOS CoP B.7)**
   Please provide me with a copy of the contract between your firm and the landowner which provides you with the authority to issue and enforce your Parking Charge Notice – Notice to Keeper.

6. **Signage**

   Please provide me with photographs of the signs you display and rely on as evidence that a lawful and legally enforceable contract has been entered in to and subsequently breached.

Please also ensure that the photographs clearly show the terms and conditions, a diagram showing the location of all of the signs around the car park and that the wording is plain and clear in sufficiently large print for a driver to understand at the car park entrance.

Summary

I look forward to receiving your acknowledgement within 14 days and your reply in full within 35 days (in accordance with the BPA AOS Code of Practice B.22.8), subject to there being no 'exceptional circumstances'. I shall then be able to make an informed decision in how I choose to respond with your Parking Charge Notice – Notice to Keeper.

If you choose to reject this challenge or fail to address the issues I have raised and seek to address, please ensure that you enclose all the required information in accordance with the BPA AOS Code of Practice 22.12 (including the necessary 'POPLA code') so that I can refer this matter to them for consideration.

I shall lodge a formal complaint to the DVLA Data Sharing Policy Group, D16 if you fail to follow any of the procedures outlined in the BPA AOS Code of Practice or your legal requirements under the Protection of Freedom Acts, or the requirements of the Practice Direction on Pre-Action Conduct.

If you insist on taking this matter further, I must inform you that I shall claim my expenses from you and my time spent at the Court rate of £X per hour. The expenses I may claim for are not exhaustive and may include stationery, travel expenses and legal fees. By continuing to pursue me, you agree to pay these costs in full.

Please Note: I wish to put you on notice that you do not have my permission to disclose or refer this letter or any other communications from me to any other individual or organisation. The only exception to this is if you specifically request permission and I provide it.

Yours faithfully

If your initial appeal fails, you can request a formal appeal with the parking firm's trade association if they are a member of the British Parking Association (BPA) or the Independence Parking Committee (IPC).

Parking on Private Land Appeals (PoPLA) is the independent body set up by the BPA for its members, and you have 28 days to lodge an appeal.

You have 21 days to lodge an appeal with the Independent Appeals Service, which is similar to PoPLA.

The odds are in your favour with appeals made with PoPLA, with a success rate of over 50% of rulings made in favour of motorists.

CHAPTER 5 – INVITATION TO TREAT

Private parking revolves around contract law and precedents set, hence why you need to understand this concept as a technicality to cancel private parking invoices.

An invitation to treat is an ancient concept in contract law which translates in to inviting you to make an offer. This is generally used by retailers so they cannot be held liable for mistakes on advertised prices, although it remains the cornerstone within contract law. Adverts are not offers and they are merely an 'invitation to treat', which translates in to you being invited to make an offer.

The retailer is not compelled to sell the goods at the price advertised. An offer is made when you present the goods to the shopkeeper, they tell you the price and you pay it.

The same notion is applied to private parking tickets.

There must be an offer, an acceptance, an intention to create a contract and consideration in order to create a legally binding contract.

An offer is an invitation communicated by one party to another to enter in to negotiations with the intention of creating a contract.

An invitation to treat is simply an indication that someone is prepared to receive offers with the view of creating a legally binding contract.

All of the terms and conditions have to be clear before and at the time a contract is entered in to and acceptance is made. Furthermore, there has to be a contract between the landowner and the parking firm for a valid contract to be upheld. Otherwise, it can be argued that the signs are simply an 'invitation to treat' and not legally binding.

The case of 'Thornton v Shoe Lane Parking Limited (1970)' is used as a prime example of stating that a clause cannot be included in to a contract after it has been finalised.

The points made here is that Mr Thornton paid for a ticket and parked his car. The ticket stated that *'this ticket is issued subject to the conditions of issue as displayed on the premises'*. There was a list of conditions on a car park pillar near the ticket machine, one of which excluded liability for *'injury to the customer howsoever that loss, misdelivery, damage or injury shall be caused'*.

Mr Thornton had an accident 3 hours later before getting in to his car and he tried to sue the car park operator. The car park operator's defence was that this was clearly stated in the contract that Mr Thornton had chosen to enter in to.

The key point that the judge made here is that customers need to be given better notice of various complex clauses made before they enter in to a contract and buy a parking ticket. Furthermore, conditions cannot be incorporated in to a contract after it has been concluded.

Once you have bought and paid for a parking ticket or entered in to a private car park, the contract is a done deal. Conditions cannot be attached to the contract afterwards.

CHAPTER 6 – HOW TO WIN YOUR APPEAL

You need to follow the correct appeals process, use the right jargon and stick strictly to the correct appeal decisions. Use legal arguments instead of mitigating circumstances. A well-structured, solid and clear case from the outset will give you a distinct advantage.

Most private parking tickets are not issued properly anyway, so the odds are in your favour if you know what to do.

The key to winning your appeal is based on two counts;

Balance of probabilities
Beyond reasonable doubt

You need to prove 'on the balance of probabilities' and 'beyond reasonable doubt' that you are in the right. You therefore need to ensure that the evidence you gather and present to support your case does just that and casts doubts on the case against you.

Remember that the onus is on the parking firm to prove that you have breached the contract, and not you to prove otherwise. This is otherwise known as a reverse burden of proof.

Any direct appeals to parking firms may be rejected because the private parking ticket firms are in business to make money and there is a clear conflict of interest. You may get it cancelled if you put a clear and convincing case forward as the parking firm may not wish to incur additional costs if your case goes to appeal.

They should respond within 7 days. You then have 28 days to take your case to appeal to Parking on Private Land Appeals (PoPLA).

Follow up to the parking firm with a phone call if you have not received a response, as it has been known for them to deny having had any contact from the motorist within 28 days. This results in you not being able to make an appeal.

If you have to ring them, ask for a PoPLA code and escalate it immediately as the PoPLA codes have an expiry date as well.

Appeals made to the International Parking Community (IPC) Independent Appeals Service (IAS) need to be done within 21 days of your initial appeal being rejected by the parking company.

Appeals are free if they are made within 21 days, although appeals can be made afterwards up to 12 months and costs £15. The results are binding on you and the parking firm.

CHAPTER 7 – THE DIFFERENCE BETWEEN DEBT COLLECTORS AND BAILIFFS

Debt collectors are not bailiffs and have no powers to seize goods to settle payment of outstanding invoices. Debt collectors are either acting on behalf of the parking firm as a subsidiary or they have purchased the alleged debt from the parking firm.

The use various intimidating tactics including writing letters in red ink and block capitals, using legalese jargon and other unsavoury methods to force you to pay the outstanding invoice.

They cannot take away your property, they must tell you when they plan to visit, they can only phone, write or visit to discuss settling the alleged debt and they cannot repeatedly contact you or harass you during unsocial hours

A bailiff has powers to seize goods to settle outstanding debts. However, this can only be done once they have been appointed by a County Court to recover a debt. A parking firm needs to take you to Court, prove the debt and you have failed to settle it.

CHAPTER 8 – COURT HEARINGS

Fail to prepare, prepare to fail is the mantra.

Do not ignore Court papers as the private parking firm will record a default judgement against you and will try to recover the money. This will also affect your credit record.

If a private parking firm makes a claim against you that goes to hearing, ensure you question their representative's right of audience. They often use third party legal firms which can result in the case being struck out before the case is even heard.

The private parking firm may even drop the claim if they can see that your evidence is watertight and may settle out of Court.

If you are representing yourself, you are referred to as 'litigant in person'.

Right of Audience
The first thing you do is question whether the solicitor who is representing the private parking firm has a right of audience.

You are asking if this person has the right to conduct legal proceedings in Court on behalf of the private parking firm.

If an individual does not have right of audience, they cannot conduct Court proceedings in Court and it is illegal to do so. This offence carries a sentence of up to 2 years in prison and / or a fine.

Barristers have right of audience in every Court and solicitors generally have right of audience in Magistrates and County Courts.

A lay representative may represent an individual who is involved in legal proceedings (otherwise known as a litigant in person) with the litigant present. A lay representative is someone who is able to represent the litigant and convey the facts better than the litigant could themselves.

Parking firms frequently rely on networks of legal advocates to represent them in the County Court. These legal advocates in turn engage with self-employed individuals who are not qualified barristers or solicitors, therefore do not have automatic right of audience. Furthermore, because they are self-employed there is no employer or disciplinary body for them to be reported to if they were found to be acting inappropriately.

Top Tips for Presenting Your Case in Court
Make sure you have a pen and paper so you can take notes. This is essential as you cannot rely on memory alone in these scenarios.

Keep all of your evidence, even if you do not think it is relevant. Phone calls recorded on a dashcam can count as evidence.

Be prepared and do your homework.

Have your answers ready for any facts that you may expect to be raised that can damage your case. Try and raise these before the other party does so you can discuss and dismiss them concisely as part of your strategy.

Ensure that your case papers are organised. Put everything in to a lever arch file with dividers in the following format:

- Court applications, orders and hearing notices
- Witness statements of evidence
- Expert reports
- Correspondence
- Notes

Take everything to Court and keep it all in one file for ease of reference.

You cannot rely on any documents that have not been filed with the Court and whatever you do rely on has to be disclosed in advance.

Stick to the facts and remain calm, polite and courteous to all parties.

Practice and polish your script so that you present your case in a compelling and convincing manner.

You may even wish to attend Court in the public gallery to see how a case is conducted as part of your preparations.

CHAPTER 9 – HOW TO SUE A PARKING FIRM

You may wish to take legal action against the parking firm for harassment and misusing your data under the General Data Protection Regulation Act 2018. Examples of this may be where your data has been disclosed to third parties without your consent and when the data shared was not accurate.

The basic Data Protection principles are as follows:

Used fairly and lawfully
Used for limited, specifically stated purposes
Used in a way that is adequate, relevant and not excessive
Accurate
Kept for no longer than is absolutely necessary
Handled according to people's data protection rights
Kept safe and secure

You are entitled to compensation if your data is misused and causes you distress.

You can refer to the Ferguson -v- British Gas case as discussed in the paragraph 'What to do if your case has been passed to debt collectors' with reference to your rights under the Protection from Harassment Act 1997.

You, as the claimant, need to evidence that the defendant 'ought to know' that their actions and conduct is likely to be construed as unreasonable harassment and would cause alarm and distress.

You can lodge a counterclaim for damages under the Protection from Harassment Act 1997 and use all correspondence and threatening letters as evidence.

If you have any disabilities or what is defined as a protected characteristic, you can also rely on the Equality Act 2010 as the parking firm needs to demonstrate that they have made reasonable adjustments and allowances for this.

Calculate your time spent dealing with this at a professional hourly rate and add on what you consider is reasonable for the alarm and distress caused to compensate you.

Private parking firms contact the DVLA and access the registered keeper database so they can send a Notice to Keeper to request payment for a parking charge. This is done on the assumption that the keeper knows that they were the driver or who was the driver.

Parking firms sign up and agree to the KADOE (Keeper at Date of Event) contract to access the DVLA registered keeper database to enforce outstanding parking charges. The KADOE contract has specific conditions attached for parking firms to access the DVLA database.

These include;

The parking firm seeks recovery in accordance with the Accredited Trade Association Code of Practice

Recovery is made from:

The driver, or

The keeper if the procedure in Schedule 4 of the Protection of Freedoms Act is used (only applies in England and Wales)

The data is only used in connection with the specific date, incident and purpose intended and is not re-used for other unrelated purposes

The parking firm has sufficient evidence to justify and demonstrate that it has reasonable cause to request the data

The data matches the information in the request for payment and that there are no discrepancies

The parking firm will adhere to the Office of Fair Trading (OFT) Debt Collection Guidance rules

There have been cases where parking firms have been proved to have altered evidence to prove their case (changing timestamps on photos). This would be a clear Data Protection breach as they have misused your data to fraudulently obtain monies by deception.

Automatic Number Plate Recognition (ANPR) is often relied on by parking firms to issue tickets and they are not foolproof. An unintentional breach of Data Protection is no defence. The parking firm as the data controller is responsible for ensuring that the data is obtained and processed for lawful purposes.

If a ticket is issued within a grace period as permitted by the BPA and IPC, then it is not only invalid but it is a clear Data Protection breach as they have unlawfully obtained your data to issue a ticket. This also breaches the KADOE contract and Code of Practice.

If you have volunteered who the driver was, the parking firms will seek to clarify the driver's details so they can send a Notice to Driver.

If the parking firm cannot identify who the driver of the vehicle was and the keeper refuses to disclose who the driver was and pay the ticket, any continuation of correspondence being sent to the keeper (and processing of the keeper's data) is a clear breach of the Act.

You have won your appeal, for example, with PoPLA and you continue receiving threatening letters. Your data is being misused unfairly and unlawfully and that in itself is a clear breach.

Can you evidence any clear breaches within the paperwork to say that your personal data (which belongs to you) has been misused without your knowledge or consent?

Has the parking firm met all of the requirements stated in the GDPR Act 2018, particularly for specified and lawful purposes only?

If the parking firm has not met all of the requirements in the GDPR Act 2018, you can demonstrate that there is 'no reasonable cause' and therefore they have breached it and misused your data.

Any mistakes in the parking ticket invalidates the contract you are claimed to have entered in to, therefore there would be no breach or misuse of your data.

You are well within your rights to report any breaches to the DVLA, although in reality this will achieve nothing and you would be better off reporting breaches to the Information Commissioner's Office (ICO) as the watchdog with oversight for data protection.

CHAPTER 10 – GENERAL DATA PROTECTION REGULATION ACT 2018

The Data Protection Act 1998 (2002 in the Isle of Man) was replaced and harmonised by the General Data Protection Regulation Act (GDPR) on 25 May 2018 and controls how your personal information is used by organisations, businesses and the Government.

The reason for this is because of technological and digital advances that were not relevant or covered in the old legislation and to harmonise and empower EU citizens with more powers over the use of their personal data.

This legislation has been in the making since 2012 and is so complex, it will be virtually impossible to unwind and will remain in place after the UK has left the EU for many years to come.

The principles remain the same and gives you the right to know what data is being held on you, and it also applies the rules for companies to adhere to when they handle and retain your data with a new accountability requirement. The GDPR requires organisations to evidence how they have complied with the principles – for example by documenting the decisions taken about a processing activity.

This legislation applies to the processing of personal data by controllers and processors in the EU regardless of whether the processing takes place in the EU or not.

The penalties for non-compliance can range up to €20m or 4% of annual global turnover, whichever is higher, and the Information Commissioner's Office (ICO) take a variety of factors in to account including the gravity of the offence, damage to the individual, if the infringement has been disclosed to the ICO and other aspects.

It is worth knowing that it is mandatory for any organisation to report any infringements of the GDPR Act 2018 to the ICO, and non-compliance and not reporting the infringement will be taken more seriously with the penalties incurred to reflect that.

You have a right to request what data any company holds about you, and this data belongs to you under the GDPR Act 2018.

The records can be in paper or electronic form as well as CCTV footage. As this can be used to identify you as an individual, the personal record belongs to you.

To access this data, you need to submit a Data Subject Access Request (DSAR) and Article 15 gives you the right to request information about your personal data that is held by a company.

Some data can be withheld in scenarios where you may be investigated for a crime, when accessing data of a deceased relative or when it could be used to identify someone who wishes to remain anonymous.

A data controller is an individual who (either alone, jointly or in common with other individuals) determines the purposes for which, and the manner in which, any personal data is processed.

A data subject is usually the consumer/customer or an employee within an organisation.

Everyone responsible for using data has to strictly adhere to Article 5 of the GDPR Act 2018 which requires that personal data shall be:

processed lawfully, fairly and in a transparent manner in relation to individuals;

collected for specified, explicit and legitimate purposes and not further processed in a manner that is incompatible with those purposes; further processing for archiving purposes in the public interest, scientific or historical research purposes or statistical purposes shall not be considered to be incompatible with the initial purposes;

adequate, relevant and limited to what is necessary in relation to the purposes for which they are processed;

accurate and, where necessary, kept up to date; every reasonable step must be taken to ensure that personal data that are inaccurate, having regard to the purposes for which they are processed, are erased or rectified without delay;

kept in a form which permits identification of data subjects for no longer than is necessary for the purposes for which the personal data are processed; personal data may be stored for longer periods insofar as the personal data will be processed solely for archiving purposes in the public interest, scientific or historical research purposes or statistical purposes subject to implementation of the appropriate technical and organisational measures required by the GDPR in order to safeguard the rights and freedoms of individuals;

processed in a manner that ensures appropriate security of the personal data, including protection against unauthorised or unlawful processing and against accidental loss, destruction or damage, using appropriate technical or organisational measures.

It is worth remembering that many firms have a standard advisory notice at the start of each telephone call when you speak to them saying, *"All calls are recorded for training and quality purposes".*

In the event that you are in dispute with a firm that states this on their telephone calls, you are entitled to a copy of the taped recorded calls under the GDPR Act 2018, which in reality, is very difficult and costly for firms to trace.

I would even go as far as to say that the majority of phone calls are not recorded at all so, more often than not, any request for a copy of any tapes that do not exist will elicit a goodwill gesture payment without any admission of liability to close the case.

You can submit a request free of charge using a standard template and the recipient has one month to comply with the request from the date of receipt (send by recorded delivery first class), otherwise they are in breach of the GDPR Act 2018 and you can lodge a complaint with the Information Commissioner's Office (ICO). This is shorter than the previous 40-day timeframe, although companies are allowed to extend this for another 2 months if the request is complicated. The company must inform you within one month if a decision is made to extend the timeframe and explain why the extension is necessary.

Data Subject Access Requests can be refused if your request is considered unfounded or excessive and the data controller is entitled to charge a fee if it can be justified for a time-consuming request.

The ICO is the regulatory body that enforces compliance with the Data Protection Act in the UK. The Isle of Man Information Commissioner (formerly the Office of the Data Protection Registrar) enforces the legislation in the Isle of Man.

You need to take the following steps before you submit a Data Subject Access Request:

- Identify who to send your request to at a company
- Consider what personal data you are seeking
- State clearly what you want
- Give your full name, date of birth and contact details
- Any information the company will need to identify you
- Specific dates to narrow the search if necessary
- Keep copies of all correspondence and proof of recorded delivery

A basic template to access your personal data in the UK and the Isle of Man is as follows:

Dear Sir / Madam,

DATA SUBJECT ACCESS REQUEST

I write to you to request that you provide the data you hold about me that I am entitled to under the General Data Protection Regulation Act 2018.

The details to enable you to identify the information I require is:

Name:
Address:
Date of Birth:
Dates:

Please advise me as soon as possible if you need any more data from me or a fee to proceed with my request, which requires you to respond to my request within one calendar month.

If you do not normally deal with these requests, please pass this letter to your Data Protection Officer or nominated staff member. The Information Commissioner's Office can assist you if you need any advice or guidance, and their website is www.ico.org.uk.

Yours faithfully,

A template to access your personal data in the UK for double dip disputes with private parking operators is as follows:

Dear Sir / Madam,

DATA SUBJECT ACCESS REQUEST

I write to you to request that you provide the data you hold about me that I am entitled to under the General Data Protection Regulation Act 2018.

The details to enable you to identify the information I require is:

Name:
Address:
Date of Birth:
Dates:
My vehicle registration:

In particular, could you include any time and date captures relating to my vehicle AND also any still picture CCTV photo captures of my vehicle from your systems. Please include copies of any correspondence to me or any third parties.

Yours faithfully,

CHAPTER 11 – HOW TO FILE A SMALL CLAIM IN COURT

This should be a last resort in any jurisdiction, and you ('the claimant') will need to evidence that you have taken all necessary steps and explored all options to resolve your dispute before you proceed, otherwise it could jeopardise the outcome.

This is referred to as 'Pre-Action Protocols', whereby you have sent a letter with sufficient information about your situation and have given the defendant a reasonable opportunity to resolve the dispute.

Alternatives to proceeding with a Small Claim include Alternative Dispute Resolution (ADR) and mediation. The method you opt for to resolve your dispute will depend on:

- the nature of the problem
- the outcome you are seeking
- how you want to resolve your dispute
- how flexible the other party is to resolve the dispute

It can be quicker, cheaper and less stressful and the concept is that both parties resolve their differences and come to an agreement.

Mediation cannot be used in a small claim.
Mediation is voluntary and a confidential form of ADR. An independent, impartial individual ('the mediator') will assist you in finding a solution that is acceptable to everyone.

A mediator can talk to both parties, separately or together, and does not make judgements or decide the outcome of a dispute.

A mediator will:

- ask questions to uncover the underlying issues
- assist the parties to understand the problems
- help each party to clarify the options for resolving their differences and dispute

Judges (Sheriffs in Scotland and Deemsters in the Isle of Man) expect you to have considered ADRs and mediation before you start a Court action.

Ombudsman Schemes are free for consumers (although traders have to pay), and cover:

- providers of financial services
- retailers, including online retailers
- energy firms
- telephone and internet providers
- furniture removal firms

You need to use the trader's internal complaints service before proceeding with a complaint with an Ombudsman.

The Consumer Ombudsman deals with all complaints outside of the remit of any other Ombudsman.

If you choose to proceed with a small claim, here are some points to consider when you are preparing your submission:

- Be specific, stick to the facts and do not waffle
- Focus on the the dispute, what you have done to try and resolve it and the result you are seeking

Do not start sentences with:

"I feel"
"I believe"
"In my opinion"

What you feel, believe and have an opinion on has no bearing on the facts of the case. Generally speaking, Courts favour the underdog on disputes with big companies so you need to tilt your case with a slant that you have acted reasonably, tried everything to resolve your dispute and have been badly treated.

You are entitled to claim for Court fees and any out-of-pocket expenses incurred – keep all receipts.

England and Wales

You can file a claim online with HM Courts and Tribunal Service in the event that you have exhausted all other avenues and cannot resort to an Ombudsman to resolve your complaint (for example, a rejected warranty claim for a scooter).

The Money Claim Online (MCOL) is the online service for claimants and defendants for HM Courts and Tribunal Service, and is a convenient and secure way of making or responding to a claim online.

MCOL is designed to be a straightforward way of submitting a County Court claim for a fixed sum of money.

Any claim using MCOL must be:

- for a fixed amount of money less than £100,000
- against no more than two defendants (people or companies)
- served to a defendant or defendants with an address in England or Wales

You cannot use MCOL if you are:

- under 18 as minors are deemed unable to enter in to contracts and therefore disputes and claims
- eligible for legal aid or help with fees
- making a claim for compensation for an accident or injury
- banned by the Court from making claims because you are a 'vexatious litigant' who uses Court cases to harass other people

You cannot use MCOL to make a claim against:

- anyone under 18 for the same reasons above
- someone who lacks 'mental capacity' and is unable to make their own decisions
- Government departments
- anyone as a result of a tribunal award
- tenancy deposit disputes that fall under the Tenancy Deposit Scheme

The defendant has 14 days to respond from the 'date of service', which is 5 days after a claim has been started and issued.

The defendant must respond to any claim within the specific timeframe with a variety of options including:

Acknowledgement of Service. This indicates that the defendant intends to contest your claim and extends the time to respond from 14 days to 28 days from the 'date of service'

States paid defence. The defendant states that the claim has been paid, and you are given the opportunity to either proceed or withdraw your claim

Full defence. The defendant disputes the full amount of the claim counterclaim. The defendant disputes the full amount of your claim and wishes to issue a counter-claim against you

Part Admission. The defendant wishes to dispute part of your claim and makes an offer to settle the dispute

Full Admission. The defendant fully admits liability and makes an offer of repayment

No response. The defendant does not respond within the allotted timeframe and you can proceed with enforcement and apply for a 'warrant of control' under certain circumstances

Payment. The defendant fully pays you the money owed direct to you

The website is www.moneyclaim.gov.uk and you need to register as an individual to proceed or respond to a claim.

Scotland

Scotland has its own distinct legal system separate from England and Wales, with Sheriffs acting as Judges and small claims being heard in Sheriff Courts.

You can file a claim online with the Scottish Courts and Tribunals where the value of a claim is up to and including £3,000.

You do not need to instruct a solicitor to proceed with a claim, although you can do so if you wish.

The process and framework is broadly similar to that outlined for small claims in England and Wales.

A small claim is usually held in a Sheriff Court within your locality (Sheriffdom). You can use a Sheriff Court in the area where the trader has its business in Scotland if you wish.

There are 39 Sheriff Courts in Scotland across 6 Sheriffdoms.

The main benefit is that you can claim an exemption from Court fees and proceed with a small claim if you are in receipt of:

- income support
- income based jobseekers' allowance
- tax credits
- certain other benefits with a disability element

You need to apply for this exemption to the Sheriff's Clerk of the Court to waive any fees before proceeding with a small claim.

The website is www.scotcourts.gov.uk

Isle of Man

The Isle of Man has its own laws, Parliament and judiciary which are entirely separate from the UK. Manx law generally follows the laws and precedents in England and Wales, but this is not exclusive and residents can only file a small claim in the Isle of Man.

You can obtain the papers to commence a claim from the public counter at the Isle of Man Courts of Justice, Bucks Road, Douglas or you can go to the website (details below) and print the forms, complete and file the papers at the public counter with the applicable fee.

You can submit a claim with the Isle of Man Courts of Justice for small claims up to and including £10,000.

One unique aspect of Manx law is that it allows you to submit small claims for personal injuries up to £5,000.

You can ask for your claim to be dealt with by the small claims procedure if the amount you are claiming for is over £10,000 provided that you have the defendant's written consent and the judge believes that your case is straightforward to proceed.

A small claim on this basis follows what is called the Small Claims Procedure.

You can make claims outside of the Isle of Man in any other jurisdiction by seeking permission from the Courts, which is considered by completing the 'Form HC8C' and filing that with your claim and fee.

Guidance notes and all forms can be found online at the Courts website, which is:

www.courts.im/courtprocedures/claims/small claims/claimant/howto.xml

CHAPTER 12 – HOW TO SEEK COMPENSATION FOR POTHOLE DAMAGE

It is fair to say that the quality of what is left of the roads on which we have the dubious pleasure of driving are atrocious, and you run the daily risk of having your suspension damaged, as well as your wheels and tyres.

This can be a costly experience and councils will make it as difficult as possible to submit claims, although I am sure that they find it cheaper to pay out compensation rather than fixing the roads in the first place.

In essence, most pothole claims result from roads that should be inspected on a regular basis, and the crux is to prove negligence either due to the defect not being noted on the last inspection, or inspections, and / or not being repaired in the appropriate timescale.

The checklist to successfully make a pothole claim is as follows:

- Contact the local authority for a claim form as soon as possible.
- Collect your evidence, again, as soon as possible. Record the date, time and place where you hit the pothole and the damage caused to your vehicle.
- Take a photo and measure the pothole's width, depth and position on the road. You may even wish to look on Google Street View, as the pothole may be clearly evidenced online well before your accident.
- Report the pothole. This can be done via www.fixmystreet.com, which is linked to local

authorities, or you can report it direct online to your local authority.

Once a pothole has been reported, the authority is on notice that they are liable for any subsequent accidents and claims until it has been fixed.

Take screenshots of the pothole using Google Earth and Google Street Maps as evidence as well. Google Street Maps has a date stamp. This can be used to prove that the local authority has not repaired a pothole for years to any sort of criteria.

I would suggest that you check to see if the pothole has been fixed 5 days after you report it and take a photo if necessary. If the pothole remains unrepaired and you have evidence to support this, it could be argued in Court that it is clear that the local authority is not reasonably maintaining the highways, and delays to repairs are a danger to life (for example, cyclists hitting a pothole at night).

What the local authority thinks is reasonable and what a Court thinks is reasonable are unlikely to be the same, and this would cast the local authority in a poor light in Court.

Complete the claim form and submit with a cover letter.

The template to submit a pothole claim is as follows:

Dear Sir/Madam

I write to you in respect of a pothole on [street name] that damaged my vehicle on [approximate time and date]. My vehicle details are [make, model and registration number] and the damage caused is [list damage].

I wish to submit a claim for the full repair costs of [amount], as you, in your capacity as the local authority, are responsible for maintaining this road.

I enclose an independent report from a reputable mechanic and garage to evidence my claim, which illustrates that:

- *The damage caused is consistent with hitting a pothole*
- *The total cost of the repairs as a result is (amount)*

I measured the pothole at that time and it measured [width], [length] and [depth]. This is clearly a danger to all road users, in particular cyclists at night, and you (as the authority responsible for maintenance) have neglected in your duty to repair it.

Your authority has a legal responsibility to maintain roads to a safe standard under the Highways Act 1980 (England and Wales) / Roads (Scotland) Act 1984, including repairing defects such as the pothole that damaged my vehicle.

Your authority also has a duty in statute to prevent road defects causing an immediate danger to road users.

I attach copies of my photos of the pothole, which clearly evidence that you have failed in your duty to maintain this road to the appropriate standard within your remit and that you are liable for the full cost of repairs to my vehicle.

Please confirm in writing that I will be reimbursed for the full costs of repairs to my vehicle as a result of your negligence. If I do not hear from you within 14 days, I shall take legal action without any further recourse to you.

I look forward to hearing from you soon.

Yours faithfully

This letter should focus the minds of the recipients, and putting them on notice that you will escalate this without any further dialogue may prompt a quick settlement.

However, you have to be prepared for a rejection and this is why you should submit a Freedom of Information (FOI) request to the local authority or Highways Agency to access the inspection logs. You need to find out how often safety inspections and road maintenance is carried out. Do not write to the claims handler as they are simply engaged by the local authority as an extra layer of bureaucracy to frustrate you and reject your claim.

Also ask for a copy of the Council's policy document for maintaining the roads direct from the local authority and the criteria for permanent and temporary pothole repairs.

Request that you want the information in a clear printed format which is easy to understand, as you may very well get a computer printout to deliberately frustrate your claim. Stick to the facts, be polite and professional and provide:

- A sketch or photocopy of a map to illustrate where the incident occurred
- A note of all costs incurred for which you are seeking compensation
- Copies of photos and receipts
- An independent mechanic's report is available if required

Keep all receipts for work done to support your claim.

You ought to be aware that whatever you say may be used in a Court of law as evidence, so be careful what you put in writing.

S58 of the Highways Act 1980 is what the councils rely on as a statutory defence if they can show that reasonable care was taken to secure the road and that it was not dangerous to traffic.

The council will probably not admit liability and will pass your claim to their insurers to reject it in due course.

This is evidenced by an article that appeared in my local press when I was writing this book, and the response you can expect to get will be similar to this:

"We write in reference to your claim and the above incident. We will offer compensation only if you can show the council legally has to. You must prove that the council was at fault.

This usually means that you need to show the council did not take reasonable care, broke a contract, or did not follow a written law.

The council must maintain certain roads and pavements. However, you are not likely to prove liability if they offer a reasonable inspection system to identify defects.

At the last inspection of this location, no defects were noted. It was not known that this had deteriorated prior to your incident occurring. Once the council were notified of this defect, they made the necessary arrangements to instruct repairs.

As the council has a reasonable inspection and repair system in place, we do not consider they can be held responsible for this accident.

We sympathise with you however we are unable to offer you compensation. If you have any other evidence that you consider will assist your claim that has not already been considered please write to us with details".

Default responses used by Claims Handlers to reject pothole claims

No reports received about the defect before the incident.

There was no defect outwith criteria at the location on the inspection before the incident.

A repair was carried out once the defect was reported but unfortunately this was after the incident.

This is the first obstacle you will be faced with. Claims handlers use these responses knowing that the majority of claimants will simply give up.

Do not act on instinct and telephone the person who wrote this letter in a fit of pique, as it will jeopardise your case. Local authorities instruct claim handlers to reject claims on the first attempt, knowing that most individuals will not pursue the matter further.

In reality, this is just the start of a claims process and you need to cast reasonable doubt on the statement that the council has a reasonable inspection and repair system in place.

You should have received all of the information that you have requested from your FOI request at this point to fire a robust counter-claim by return.

Scrutinise any discrepancies between the local authorities' road maintenance programme and the information you have from your FOI request.

If there are any discrepancies, submit your counter-claim pointing out that the local authority has failed to adhere to its own policy in adequately maintaining the road in question and that your claim is legitimate and should be honoured accordingly.

It is also worth checking other aspects of the FOI response including:

How were the inspections done?
If it was in a van, what speed was the van travelling at?
Was the inspector accompanied by a driver or was he / she alone on the inspection?
What is the history of the road in question regarding defects?

If the local authority was aware of the pothole, the questions to ask are:

How long did it take to fix the pothole once they were notified?
If the authority had not repaired the pothole, how long had they known about it before you hit it?
Was the pothole given a risk assessment and categorised?
Were adequate repairs made?

If there are no discrepancies, you are unlikely to succeed with your case.

The national standards that local authorities should adhere to can be found on this link:

http://www.ciht.org.uk/media/12297/well-maintained-highways-18-september-2013-clean.pdf

This document has 512 pages in it, but I have saved you the time and effort in trawling through it and the relevant sections for the purpose of pothole claims are as follows:

Page 110 section 9.4 states:

9.4 SAFETY INSPECTIONS

9.4.1 Safety inspections are designed to identify all defects likely to create danger or serious inconvenience to users of the network or the wider community. Such defects should include those that will require urgent attention (within 24 hours) as well as those where the locations and sizes are such that longer periods of response would be acceptable.

9.4.2 They are normally undertaken by slow moving vehicle, at frequencies that reflect the characteristics of the particular highway and its use. In busy urban areas, particularly when inspecting footways, it may be difficult to obtain the necessary level of accuracy from vehicle-based inspections and walking should be used. It would seem logical for cycle routes to be inspected by cycle, although inspection of parts of some shared routes may be possible by vehicle.

Page 112 section 9.4.9 states:
Table 4 – Safety Inspection Frequency

Feature	Description	Category	Frequency
Roads	Strategic Route	2	1 month
	Main Distributor	3(a	1 month
	Secondary Distributor	3(b)	1 month

	Link Road	4(a)	3 months
	Local Access	4(b)	1 year

The descriptions are interpreted as follows:

A strategic route is a trunk road or major 'A' road

A main distributor is a major urban road linking to trunk roads and A roads

A secondary distributor applies to urban roads and bus routes carrying local traffic

A link road applies to rural roads that links to big and small urban roads, many junctions, path access

Local access applies to roads that serve few properties with local access (housing estates, etc)

Page 113 section 9.4.17 – 18 states:
9.4.17 During safety inspections, all observed defects that provide a risk to users should be recorded and the level of response determined on the basis of risk assessment. The degree of deficiency in highway elements will be crucial in determining the nature and speed of response. Although some general guidance can be given on the likely risk associated with particular defects, on-site judgement will always need to take account of particular circumstances. For example, the degree of risk from a pothole depends upon not merely its depth but also its surface area and location.

9.4.18 This Code defines defects in two categories, which correspond with those adopted in England by the Highways Agency (HA) in respect of motorways and trunk roads:

Category 1 - those that require prompt attention because they represent an immediate or imminent hazard or because there is a risk of short-term structural deterioration.

Category 2 - all other defects.

Most potholes recorded will be Cat 2 or lower.

You need to try and evidence this and prove that the local authority did not repair it after the last inspection.

Be prepared to negotiate on any offers made to resolve your claim. You may be able to claim for additional travel expenses in the event of your vehicle being off the road. You will usually not be able to claim for any inconvenience. However, it is a variable and each situation is different. If all else fails, you can take it to the Small Claims Court but you may be liable for all costs if your claim fails.

Another alternative would be to check your car insurance policy to see if it has a 'protect your rights' clause or a free legal helpline to potentially assist with your claim.

The template to submit a pothole claim on receipt of a FOI request is as follows:

Dear Sir/Madam

I write to you in respect of a pothole on [street name] that damaged my vehicle on [approximate time and date]. My vehicle details are [make, model and registration number] and the damage caused is [list damage].

I wish to submit a claim for the full repair costs of [amount], as you, in your capacity as the local authority, are responsible for maintaining this road.

I enclose an independent report from a reputable mechanic and garage to evidence my claim, which illustrates that:

- *The damage caused is consistent with hitting a pothole*

- *The total cost of the repairs as a result is [amount]*

I also enclose photos of the damage caused by the pothole.

I measured the pothole at that time and it measured [width], [length] and [depth]. This is clearly a danger to all road users, in particular cyclists at night, and you (as the authority responsible for maintenance) neglected in your duty to repair it without delay.

I submitted a Freedom of Information (FOI) request to obtain the records from your authority in respect of the road maintenance policy and history of this road where I sustained the damage to my vehicle.

The information I have obtained evidences the following anomalies:

Your authority failed to follow the maintenance and inspection policy applicable to the road in question by [delete as appropriate]:

inspections not being carried out as often as recommended in your policy [give examples]
inspections not being enacted correctly [give details]
repairs not being made as soon as is practical after being notified

Your authority has failed to adequately follow the road maintenance and inspection policy and has not met national standards

[Note discrepancies between the local authority's policy and national standards]

Your authority has a legal responsibility to maintain roads to a safe standard under the Highways Act 1980 (England and Wales) / Roads (Scotland) Act 1984, including repairing defects such as the pothole that damaged my vehicle. Your authority also has a duty to comply with the Well-maintained Highways Code of Practice and to prevent road defects causing an immediate danger to road users.

The enclosed photos clearly evidence that you have failed in your duty to maintain this road to the appropriate standard within your remit and that you are liable for the full cost of repairs to my vehicle.

Please confirm in writing that I will be reimbursed for the full costs of repairs to my vehicle as a result of your negligence.

I look forward to hearing from you soon.

Yours faithfully

Real Life Example
I collided with some loose tarmac from a badly repaired pothole on my scooter in Edinburgh. This happened in a bus lane (we are allowed to use bus lanes up here but it's risky with cars shooting over them in to side streets, etc) on a busy main road on the outskirts of Edinburgh towards the airport. A less experienced rider would have fared much worse and I was lucky to have held it together without being thrown off my scooter.

The timeline to getting this resolved was;

Claim submitted to Edinburgh City Council on 26th February 2017
Acknowledged by the Council on 23rd March 2017 and sent to their Claims Handlers
Claims Handler confirmed receipt on 28th March 2017
Settled on 4th April 2017

It was clear to me that the Claims Handlers were going to hedge their bets on my claim, which was evidenced by this paragraph;

"If we consider that an offer of compensation should be made, we can take into account the value of the damaged items rather than the full replacement cost. If you are insured for this loss, you should contact your own insurers for advice. Their claims process is usually quicker because you do not have to establish legal liability and most insurance policies cover full replacement of damaged items".

My robust response achieved a full and final settlement within 2 working days, and I thought that adding a link to my website would be a nice touch to focus their minds.

Dear Amy,

Thank you for your email.

I wish to note that Edinburgh Council promptly 'repaired' (I use that word loosely) the pothole the day after they received my compensation claim, which speaks for itself and they certainly didn't act on it after I spoke to them to report it. They simply sent someone to clear up the loose tarmac that had been thrown out of the pothole that was not repaired properly and resulted in my accident.

You are probably aware that a main road like this should be inspected every 4 weeks and I know that a Freedom of Information (FoI) request would reveal reports that would ascertain whether Edinburgh Council has done this. I have seen better maintained farm tracks than some of the roads around Edinburgh and riding a scooter is a high-risk occupation at the best of times without having to look out for loose boulders from potholes on busy main roads.

I would hope that fairness and justice will prevail for the sake of a £85 claim and that I will be fully reimbursed and avoid the need to contest it and incur time, costs and administration at your end that will far outweigh what I have had to pay to repair my scooter.

I look forward to hearing from you in due course.

Best wishes,

Scott.

The motto here is to just cut through the legalese jargon and point out that you know that they probably haven't maintained the road properly and you will find out at substantial costs to the Council.

USEFUL CONTACTS

The contact details for the BPA are as follows:

British Parking Association
Stuart House
41-43 Perrymount Road
Haywards Heath
West Sussex
RH16 3BN

T: 01444 447 300
F: 01444 454 105
E: info@britishparking.co.uk
W: www.britishparking.co.uk

The contact details for the IPC are as follows:

The IPC
PO Box 431
Knutsford
Cheshire
WA16 1EP

T: 01565 655 467
W: www.theipc.info

Appeals can be made against operators who are members of the BPA to Parking on Private Land Appeals (PoPLA). PoPLA is an independent appeals service which is free to access and is operated by the Ombudsman Service.

Contact details are as follows:

POPLA
PO Box 1270
Warrington
WA4 9RL

T: 0330 159 6126
W: www.popla.co.uk

The IPC cannot investigate complaints about parking charges so appeals against parking charges need to be taken up with the Independent Appeals Service (IAS).

The IAS is administered by the IPC and appeals are considered by a team of Adjudicators and a Lead Adjudicator.

The Lead Adjudicator's role is to oversee the independence and integrity of the service and to assume collective responsibility for all rulings and the Adjudicators within the IAS. The Lead Adjudicator is a current solicitor or barrister and they are independent in this role.

You need to appeal with the car park operator first before you can take your appeal to the IAS which you can do online or by post.

The Independent Adjudicator is only allowed to consider whether the charge is legal or not, and they cannot consider mitigation. You can appeal on any ground which casts reasonable doubt on the legality of the charge or any aspect that affects the suggestion that you are liable for it.

The IAS accepts appeals online via their website, which is: www.theias.org

Information Commissioner's Office
Wycliffe House
Water Lane
Wilmslow
Cheshire
SK9 5AF

T: 0303 123 1113 / 01625 545 745
E: casework@ico.org.uk
W: www.ico.org.uk

Scotland
You will need to contact the Scottish Parking Appeals Service, which does not have a website.

Contact details are:

Scottish Parking Appeals Service
10 Waterloo Place
Edinburgh
EH1 3EG

T: 0131 221 0409

Information Commissioner's Office
45 Melville Street
Edinburgh
EH3 7HL
T: 0131 244 9001
E: scotland@ico.org.uk

Northern Ireland
The Consumer Council
Floor 3, Seatem House
28 – 32 Alfred Street
Belfast
BT2 8EN

T: 0800 121 6022 / 028 9025 1600
E: contact@consumercouncil.org.uk
W: www.consumercouncil.org.uk

Connect with the Author

Want to stay in touch with Scott and be the first to hear about his new books?

Social media links:

Instagram:	@thecomplaintsresolver
Twitter:	@scott_expert
Facebook:	The Complaints Resolver
Websites:	www.thecomplaintsresolver.co.uk
	www.awriterinedinburgh.com

If you enjoyed this book, don't forget to leave a review on Amazon! I highly appreciate your reviews, and it only takes a minute to do.

www.ingramcontent.com/pod-product-compliance
Lightning Source LLC
Chambersburg PA
CBHW070806220526
45466CB00002B/564